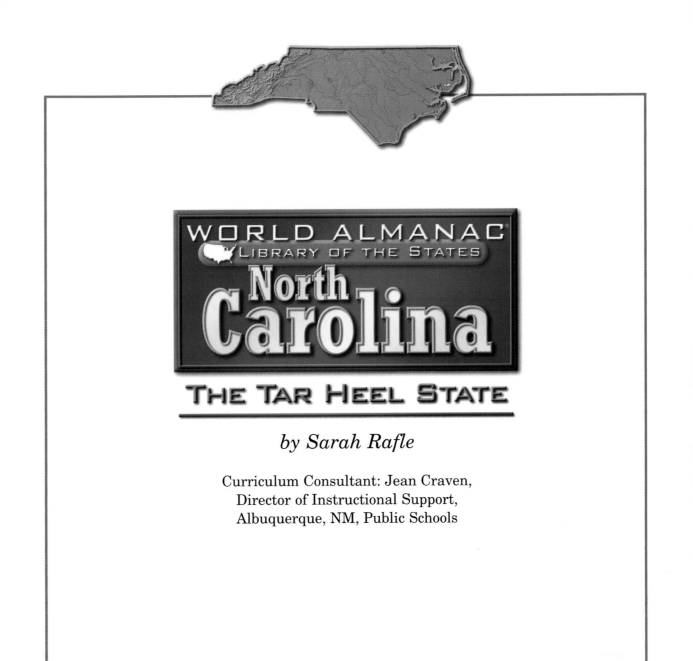

WORLD ALMANAC LIBRARY OF THE STATES

North Carolina

THE TAR HEEL STATE

by Sarah Rafle

Curriculum Consultant: Jean Craven,
Director of Instructional Support,
Albuquerque, NM, Public Schools

WORLD ALMANAC® LIBRARY

Please visit our web site at: www.worldalmanaclibrary.com
**For a free color catalog describing World Almanac® Library's list of high-quality books
and multimedia programs, call 1-800-848-2928 or fax your request to (414) 332-3567.**

Library of Congress Cataloging-in-Publication Data

Rafle, Sarah.
    North Carolina, the Tar Heel State / by Sarah Rafle.
        p. cm. — (World Almanac Library of the states)
    Includes bibliographical references and index.
    Summary: Illustrations and text present the history, geography, people, politics and
government, economy, and social life and customs of North Carolina, which was the first
colony to vote for independence.
    ISBN 0-8368-5119-6 (lib. bdg.)
    ISBN 0-8368-5289-3 (softcover)
    1. North Carolina—Juvenile literature. [1. North Carolina.] I. Title. II. Series.
F254.3.R34 2002
975.6—dc21   2001046986

This edition first published in 2002 by
World Almanac® Library
330 West Olive Street, Suite 100
Milwaukee, WI 53212 USA

This edition © 2002 by World Almanac® Library.

Design and Editorial: **Jack&Bill**/Bill SMITH STUDIO Inc.
Editors: Jackie Ball and Kristen Behrens
Art Directors: Ron Leighton and Jeffrey Rutzky
Photo Research and Buying: Christie Silver and Sean Livingstone
Design and Production: Maureen O'Connor and Jeffrey Rutzky
World Almanac® Library Editors: Patricia Lantier, Amy Stone, Valerie J. Weber,
Catherine Gardner, Carolyn Kott Washburne, Alan Wachtel, Monica Rausch
World Almanac® Library Production: Scott M. Krall, Eva Erato-Rudek, Tammy Gruenewald,
Katherine A. Goedheer

Photo credits: p. 5 © Richard T. Nowitz/CORBIS; p. 6 (all) © Corel; p. 7 © ArtToday;
p. 9 © North Carolina Museum of Art/CORBIS; p. 10 © Ramond Gehman/CORBIS;
p. 11 © Bettmann/CORBIS; p. 12 © Jo Miller; p. 13 © Corel; p. 14 © Library of Congress;
p. 15 © Library of Congress; p. 17 © ArtToday; p. 18 © PhotoDisc; p. 19 courtesy of Greater
Raleigh CVB; p. 20 (from left to right) © Glen Tig, Chapel Hill/Orange County Visitors Bureau,
© Corel; p. 22 © Corel, © PhotoDisc, © Painet; p. 23 © Hank Walker/TimePix; p. 26–27 (all)
© PhotoDisc; p. 29 courtesy of Greater Raleigh CVB; p. 30 © Corel; p. 31 (all) © Library of
Congress; p. 32 © PhotoDisc; p. 33 courtesy of Chapel Hill/Orange County Visitors Bureau;
p. 34 courtesy of North Carolina Zoological Park; p. 35 (from left to right) courtesy of Greater
Raleigh CVB, courtesy of Southern Pines CVB; p. 36 © Tami Chappel/Reuters/TimePix;
p. 37 © PhotoDisc; Dover Publications; p. 37 first flight © ArtToday; p. 38 © PhotoDisc; p. 39
(from left to right) © Library of Congress, © Artville; p. 40 (insets) © Dover Publications,
(bottom) © Library of Congress; p. 41 (top) © Herb Snitzer/TimePix, (bottom) © Artville;
p. 41–42 © Library of Congress; p. 44 © Corel; p. 45 (all) © Corel

Printed in the United States of America

1 2 3 4 5 6 7 8 9 06 05 04 03 02

North Carolina

History and Mystery

I t's 500 miles (805 kilometers) wide, and its sprawling distance, bounded by Tennessee on the west and the Atlantic Ocean on the east, is matched by North Carolina's long history — a history full of "firsts." The Wright brothers made the state "First in Flight," but way before they lifted off at Kill Devil Hills the state had been home to the first English child born in the New World, the first town named for George Washington (in 1775), and the country's first gold rush. North Carolina was the first colony to vote in favor of independence; in fact, the Charlotte Town Resolves, resolutions written in 1775 defying British rule, preceded America's own Declaration of Independence. The Resolves also showed North Carolinians' fiery, passionate spirit: "Resolved: that whoever directly or indirectly abets or in any way, form, or manner countenances the invasion of our rights as attempted by the parliament of Great Britain is an enemy to this country . . . "

Today the "Tar Heel State" leads the country in production of tobacco, textiles, and furniture. Its so-called Research Triangle — formed by the cities of Raleigh, Durham, and Chapel Hill — is a major technological center. The state's diverse geography and cultural heritage provide something for everyone, from mountains to stately homes to battleships to beaches — miles and miles of beaches that are both beautiful and deadly. Pirates once roamed the 175-mile (282-km) Outer Banks; ships were wrecked there. A little girl and her entire community once vanished from an offshore island in one of America's earliest mysteries.

For hurricanes, the North Carolina coast is a favorite place to make landfall. North Carolina's mild climate, good job opportunities, and natural beauty, however, make it a favorite destination that grows more popular every year.

▶ Map of North Carolina showing its interstate highway system, as well as major cities and waterways.

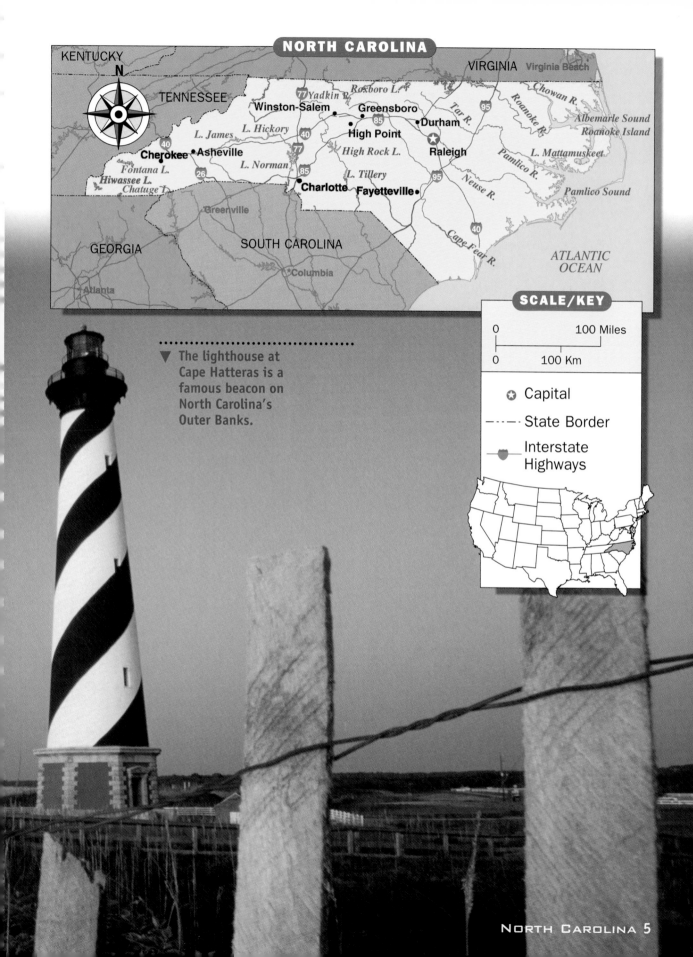

NORTH CAROLINA

KENTUCKY

VIRGINIA Virginia Beach

TENNESSEE

N

Winston-Salem Roxboro L. Yadkin R. 77

Greensboro Tar R. 95 Chowan R.

85 Durham Roanoke R.

High Point Albemarle Sound

40 Raleigh Roanoke Island

L. James L. Hickory

Cherokee •Asheville High Rock L. L. Mattamuskeet

77 Pamlico R.

Fontana L. L. Norman L. Tillery

Hiwassee L. 26 Charlotte 85 Fayetteville• 95 Pamlico Sound

Chatuge L. Neuse R.

Greenville Pamlico Sound

GEORGIA

SOUTH CAROLINA 40

Cape Fear R.

ATLANTIC
OCEAN

Columbia

Atlanta

▼ The lighthouse at
Cape Hatteras is a
famous beacon on
North Carolina's
Outer Banks.

Fast Facts

NORTH CAROLINA (NC),
The Tar Heel State (or Old North State)

Entered Union

November 21, 1789 (12th state)

Capital	Population
Raleigh	276,093

Total Population (2000)

8,049,313 (11th most populous state)

Largest Cities	Population
Charlotte	540,828
Raleigh	276,093
Greensboro	223,891
Durham	187,035
Winston-Salem	185,776

Land Area

48,711 square miles (126,161 square kilometers) (29th largest state)

State Motto

Esse Quam Videri — *Latin for "To be rather than to seem"*

State Song

"The Old North State" by William Gaston and E. E. Randolph

State Mammal

Gray Squirrel — *The squirrel feels more at home in the wilderness, but many also inhabit city parks and suburbs.*

State Dog

Plott Hound — *Originating in the mountains of North Carolina around 1750, the Plott Hound is one of only four breeds known to have developed in the United States.*

State Bird

Cardinal — *This state bird is sometimes known as the Winter Redbird. It lives in North Carolina throughout the year.*

State Fish

Channel Bass

State Reptile

Eastern Box Turtle

State Insect

Honeybee — *Every year honeybees produce more than two million dollars worth of honey in North Carolina, but they are even more valuable for their role in the pollination of crops and other plants.*

State Tree

Pine

State Flower

Dogwood

State Shell

Scotch bonnet *(pronounced bonay)*

State Gem

Emerald

State Boat

Shad Boat — *An easily maneuverable sailboat developed on North Carolina's Roanoke Island. It is named after the fish it was designed to help catch.*

Blue Ridge Parkway This scenic route connects the Great Smoky Mountains National Park in North Carolina with the Shenandoah National Park in Virginia. In North Carolina the parkway extends 252 miles (406 km), with stunning scenery along the way.

Wright Brothers National Memorial
Kill Devil Hills
On North Carolina's Outer Banks, this is the site of the first powered air flight by Wilbur and Orville Wright. For the very same reason that the Wright Brothers chose it — strong winds — the area is still popular for hang-gliding and kite flying.

Cherokee Indian Reservation *Cherokee*
Homeland of the Eastern Band of the Cherokee Indians, this reservation welcomes thousands of visitors each year.

For other places and events, see p. 44

BIGGEST, BEST, AND MOST

- Grandfather Mountain is said to be the world's oldest. It is also home to the nation's highest swinging bridge — 1 mile (1.6 km) high!

- The Biltmore Estate, in Asheville, North Carolina, boasts the largest house in the world, with 250 rooms.

- North Carolina is a leader in fine furniture production. More than 60 percent of the nation's furniture is manufactured in North Carolina.

STATE FIRSTS

- North Carolina's early settlement on Roanoke Island gave rise to many firsts, including Virginia Dare, the first child of English parents born in the Americas, and the first letter written in English in the Americas.

- The Watauga Commonwealth, established in North Carolina and Tennessee in 1772, was the first independent civil government established on the American continent.

- North Carolina is "First in Flight" — the site of the first successful flight of a heavier-than-air vehicle powered by an engine.

Tar Heels

North Carolina's first major industry was the production of naval supplies: items used in the construction and maintenance of ships. As well as lumber, the colony's seemingly endless pine forests yielded tar, pitch, and turpentine. The origin of the state's nickname — the "Tar Heel State" — is shrouded in mystery. One explanation is that it originated during a particularly brutal Civil War battle. Some Confederate troops retreated and left the North Carolina soldiers to fight Union soldiers alone. The North Carolinians threatened to put tar on the retreating soldiers' boots so that they would "stick better in the next fight."

Blackbeard

With a beard that almost covered his face, the pirate known as Blackbeard would strike terror into the hearts of his victims, according to some early accounts, by weaving wicks laced with gunpowder into his hair — and lighting them during battle! A big man, he added to his menacing appearance by wearing a crimson coat, two swords at his waist, and bandoliers stuffed with numerous weapons across his chest. He sailed the North Carolina coast for years before being killed in 1718.

The Tar Heel State

... being excited with a laudable and pious zeal for the propagation of the Christian Faith and the enlargement of our Empire and Dominions, HAVE humbly besought leave of us, by their industry and Charge, to Transport and make an ample Colony of our Subjects, Natives of our Kingdom of England and elsewhere within our Dominions, unto a certain Country, hereafter described, in the parts of AMERICA not yet cultivated or planted ...

— King Charles II, 1663

The first settlers in the region that would become North Carolina probably arrived more than five thousand years ago after migrating across North America. When the first European explorers arrived in North Carolina in the 1500s, there were an estimated 35,000 Native Americans living in the region. They were divided roughly into three regional and linguistic families corresponding to North Carolina's three main geographic areas. The most prominent tribes were the Croatoans (or Hatteras) and Roanoke on the southern coast, the Cherokee in the western mountains, and the Catawba and Tuscarora on the coastal plain and Piedmont. The Croatoan and Roanoke spoke Algonquian, the Cherokee spoke an Iroquoian dialect, and the Catawba spoke Siouan.

Native Americans of North Carolina
Catawba
Cherokee
Croatoans (Hatteras)
Roanoke
Tuscarora

European Settlements

The first known European exploration of North Carolina took place in 1524, when Giovanni da Verrazano, an Italian sea captain in the service of France, sailed along the coast. Two years later Lucas Vasquez de Ayllon of Spain is believed to have visited Cape Fear in search of a place to settle. He decided the area was unsuitable and moved farther south. In 1540 Spanish explorer Hernando de Soto and an army of six hundred men traveled from Florida to North Carolina in search of gold.

In 1584 English nobleman Sir Walter Raleigh sent his first exploring party to find a suitable site for settlement.

Captains Philip Amadas and Arthur Barlowe landed at a North Carolina island the Native Americans called "Roanoke." The island's name came from the shells Native Americans used for money, which they called "ronoak." Impressed with the island's lush forests and abundant resources, the men returned to England with news of a land where people could settle.

In 1585 the first English colony in America was established on Roanoke Island. Hardships, however, forced the settlers to return to England the following year. In 1587 Raleigh sent another expedition to Roanoke Island, under

····································
▼ *Storm Over the Blue Ridge* by William Charles Anthony Frerichs, circa 1905.

the governorship of John White. One month after the establishment of the colony, White's granddaughter, Virginia Dare, became the first child of English parents to be born on American soil. Later that year White left the 108 men, women, and children and sailed back to England for supplies. When he returned in 1590, the colony had disappeared; all that remained was the word "CROATOAN" carved on a nearby tree. The fate of little Virginia Dare and the "Lost Colony" remains a mystery.

The first Europeans to settle permanently in North Carolina came around 1650 from the colony of Virginia, where farmland was already becoming scarce. The first of these immigrants built farms in the Albemarle Sound area. By 1680 about five thousand colonists had settled in North Carolina. Although the Native Americans and early settlers had established a congenial trading system, the Tuscarora soon grew angry with the settlers for encroaching on their land. Several hundred settlers and more than one thousand Native Americans were killed between 1711 and 1713 in the bloody Tuscarora War. The surviving Tuscarora were driven out of North Carolina.

▼ The last remains of the "Lost Colony's" earthen fort, built in 1585 by John White's expedition.

While conflict with the Native Americans increased inland, residents on North Carolina's coast contended with pirates. Violence persisted along the coast until 1718, when ships were sent out against the pirates.

Revolution

In 1712 the colony known as Carolina was divided into North and South Carolina. In 1729 the proprietors sold the colonies back to King George II, making them royal colonies. North Carolina thrived as a royal colony as a result of wise government and rich natural resources. By 1775 the population of North Carolina had increased from 36,000 to 350,000, with settlement spreading westward across the Piedmont and into the western mountains.

In the years immediately preceding the Revolutionary War, however, North Carolinians were at war with themselves. The rich plantation owners on the eastern coast dominated the political scene and gave the small farmers in the Piedmont region little say in government and taxation. Angered by this, a group of farmers calling themselves the Regulators vowed to "regulate public grievances and abuses of power." It took Royal Governor William Tryon and one thousand troops to defeat the Regulators at the Battle of Alamance Creek in 1771.

By the mid-1760s England began levying taxes on Americans to help finance other colonial wars. The Stamp Act forced colonists throughout America to buy tax stamps for items such as legal documents and newspapers. Colonial protesters called the Sons of Liberty led demonstrations and armed rebellions against these taxes.

In North Carolina the Revolutionary War began as a battle between patriots (or Whigs) in

Virginia Dare and the Lost Colony

Theories to explain the disappearance of Virginia Dare and the rest of the Roanoke Island Colony have ranged from massacre by Spaniards or Native Americans to disease, starvation, or assimilation into Indian tribes. Recently scientists have proposed another explanation: The Lost Colony fell prey to the region's worst drought in eight centuries. Researchers came to this conclusion by analyzing tree rings from an eight hundred-year-old bald cypress. Their findings suggest "extraordinary drought" at the time the colony vanished. A drought could have killed all the crops, causing starvation or a mass movement to a more welcoming location.

favor of independence from England, and loyalists (or
Tories) who remained loyal to the crown. In February 1776
patriot forces triumphed over the loyalists at the Battle of
Moore's Creek Bridge. The victory prevented the British
from commandeering the port of Wilmington and invading
North Carolina. On April 12, 1776, the state made history
by becoming the first colony to instruct its delegates to the
Continental Congress to vote for separation from England.

Toward the end of the Revolutionary War, a key battle
again was fought in North Carolina. The Battle of Guilford
Courthouse took place in what is now Greensboro on March
15, 1781. The battle significantly weakened the English
army. Because of its heavy losses at Guilford Courthouse,
the British lost the war's last big battle at Yorktown,
Virginia, in October 1781.

North Carolina was also influential in the creation of a
Bill of Rights. The state refused to ratify the United States
Constitution without amendments protecting freedom of
speech and other basic rights. In November 1789, North
Carolina approved the Constitution with its Bill of Rights
and became the twelfth state. In 1794 Raleigh became the
state capital, named after Sir Walter Raleigh.

Forced Out

In May 1775 the people
of Charlotte issued a
declaration called the
Charlotte Town Resolves,
protesting Great Britain's
"unjust and arbitrary
Pretensions with
Respect to America."
Historians disagree as to
whether a "Declaration
of Independence" was
also issued at Charlotte
in May 1775.

Stuck in Time

During the early 1800s it seemed as if North Carolina was stuck in its own tar. The state was known as the "Rip Van Winkle State" after the fictional man who slept for twenty years. While its neighbors Virginia and South Carolina were centers of wealth and prestige, progress seemed to pass North Carolina by.

The population of North Carolina declined from third in the nation in 1790 to seventh by 1840. As settlers moved westward through North Carolina, they encountered native Cherokee lands. In the 1830s, to alleviate conflict and make room for settlers throughout the eastern United States, the federal government relocated the Cherokee and other eastern tribes to lands west of the Mississippi River. The Native Americans were forced to walk more than 1,000 miles (1,609 kilometers) from North Carolina to what is now Oklahoma. Nearly one-quarter died of starvation, sickness, and exposure on what survivors called the "Trail of Tears."

Getting Stronger

In 1835 revisions to the state constitution stimulated business and gave new political strength to the people of western North Carolina. Better transportation was a high priority, which the government addressed by chartering companies to build a network of plank roads across the state. These roads became known as "farmers' railroads" since they enabled farmers to transport their goods to market. In 1840 the state's first actual railroad line was completed. North Carolina had awakened.

In the years before the Civil War, about 30 percent of North Carolina's population was black, but slavery was not as firmly entrenched as in other southern states. In fact, antislavery sentiment was strong until about 1830. Lunsford Lane, a former slave who purchased his and his family's freedom, was one of the antislavery movement's most powerful voices. Attitudes changed, however, following a rebellion in 1831 led by Nat Turner, a slave in Virginia. Afraid of a slave revolution, North Carolinians passed harsh laws concerning slaves and forced freed blacks to wear badges to distinguish them from slaves.

Edenton Tea Party

Many women took the lead in the boycott of English goods. On October 25, 1774, Penelope Barker gathered fifty-one women from Edenton, North Carolina, to sign a document supporting the struggle for independence. They pledged to support their Boston cousins in opposition to British taxes on tea by no longer using East India Tea. This was one of the earliest organized efforts on the part of women to influence public policy. In the eighteenth century, politics was thought to be an improper arena for women, but women's public influence did increase with the American Revolution.

Civil War

In the period leading up to the Civil War, North Carolinians once again found themselves divided. Based on their attitudes towards slavery, people in the East largely supported a Confederacy (the South: pro-slavery), while most in the western mountains favored the Union (the North: anti-slavery). Because of this division, North Carolina was the last Southern state to secede from the Union. Of the approximately 125,000 North Carolinians who fought for the Confederacy, about 40,000 died. This was the highest death toll of any Confederate state. About one-quarter of all Confederate soldiers killed came from North Carolina.

Of the nearly one hundred battles fought in the state, the biggest and bloodiest was the Battle of Bentonville on March 19–21, 1865. Shortly after losing this battle, the Confederates lost the Civil War. The end of the war signaled the end of slavery, the solidification of the Union, and the beginning of the Reconstruction period. North Carolinians rejoined the Union in 1868 and quickly rebuilt their state.

Trail of Tears

Disputes between the U.S. government and Native peoples over land in North Carolina and neighboring regions led to what became known as the "Trail of Tears." Federal troops forced some fifteen thousand Cherokees to relocate in Oklahoma. During this more than 1,000-mile-(1,609-km-)long march, about four thousand Cherokees died.

▼ The U.S.S. *Commodore Barney* patrolled North Carolina's inland rivers during the Civil War.

Reconstruction and the Twentieth Century

The period of Reconstruction in North Carolina saw great growth in manufacturing. Rather than continuing to send their natural resources to other states to be made into finished products, North Carolinians built their own cotton mills and furniture factories. By 1900 the Tar Heel State led the nation in the production of textiles and furniture.

On December 17, 1903, Orville and Wilbur Wright made the first airplane flight in history at Kill Devil Hills in North Carolina's Outer Banks. This event put North Carolina on the international map and led to the state's proud claim as "First in Flight."

The Wright Brothers' invention led to the development of military airplanes, which were very valuable during World War I. About 100,000 North Carolinians served in World War I. Textile workers in the state produced clothing for the U.S. armed forces in both World War I and World War II. Nearly 400,000 Tar Heels served in World War II.

Although North Carolina enjoyed tremendous economic prosperity following World War II, racial inequality and injustice also prevailed. In protest against segregation of public spaces, four black college students staged the first "sit-in" at the Woolworth's lunch counter in Greensboro on February 1, 1960. They refused to leave unless served. This milestone in the Civil Rights Movement led to the integration of public facilities and the repeal of laws aimed at keeping blacks from voting. In 1964 the Civil Rights Act banned the segregation of public facilities.

In 1959 the Research Triangle Park was established by leading research universities — the University of North Carolina at Chapel Hill, Duke University, and North Carolina State University — to enhance and support North Carolina's economic growth. This huge research complex in the Raleigh-Durham area has brought together major corporations and the area's leading universities to conduct specialized research. The complex has made North Carolina a national research center. Such innovations as Astroturf and AIDS medicines occurred inside Research Triangle Park. In 1965 IBM was one of the first companies to locate within the complex.

▼ After being refused service at a Woolworth's lunch counter in Greensboro, students from North Carolina Agricultural and Technical College staged a sitdown strike. Today the lunch counter is in the collection of the Smithsonian's National Museum of American History, in Washington, D.C.

Tar Heelers

> In Short I never saw a people seemed to me to be
> so really happy as our Countrymen there.
>
> — *Campbell of Balliol, Letter to Scotland, 1772*

North Carolina ranks eleventh in population and is one of the fastest-growing among the fifty states. In 2000 North Carolina had 8,049,313 people, compared with 6,628,637 in 1990. This increase is largely the result of migration from other states. North Carolina's flourishing industries, pleasant climate, and excellent employment opportunities attract many people.

In North Carolina, about half of the population lives in rural areas, a higher proportion than in many states. Agriculture is a major business and employer, and many people still run small farms, much as their ancestors did. "Cottage" industries, producing traditional handmade crafts, flourish in the western mountains of the state. An increasing number of people, however, are moving from the mountains and farmlands to the cities to join the workforce in the state's thriving industries. The greatest concentration of urban dwellers is in the industrialized Piedmont region at

Age Distribution in North Carolina

0–4	539,509
5–19	1,653,851
20–24	577,508
25–44	2,500,535
45–64	1,808,862
65 and over	969,048

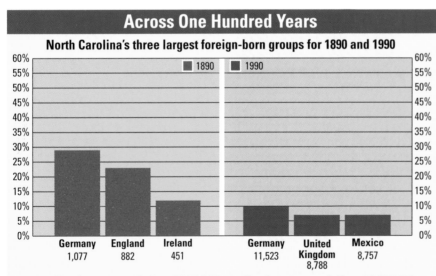

Across One Hundred Years

North Carolina's three largest foreign-born groups for 1890 and 1990

■ 1890   ■ 1990

Germany	England	Ireland
1,077	882	451

Total state population: 1,617,947
Total foreign-born: 3,871 (0.2%)

Germany	United Kingdom	Mexico
11,523	8,788	8,757

Total state population: 10,847,115
Total foreign-born: 115,077 (1%)

Patterns of Immigration

The total number of people who immigrated to North Carolina in 1998 was 6,415. Of that number, the largest immigrant groups were from Mexico (13%), India (9%), and China (5%).

the state's center. Charlotte is North Carolina's largest city, with a population of 540,828. The state's other major cities, in order of population, are Raleigh, Greensboro, Durham, and Winston-Salem.

Before the first settlers came to North Carolina in the 1500s, some thirty different Native American tribes lived in the state. As the Europeans ventured westward, conflicts broke out resulting in the Tuscarora War and later the Trail of Tears. Today there are approximately eighty thousand Native Americans living in North Carolina, accounting for a little over 1 percent of the population. About eight thousand live on the Qualla-Cherokee Indian Reservation, which is located west of Asheville in the state's western mountains.

More immigrants have come to North Carolina from other states than from other countries. Nearly all of the state's residents were born in the United States. Most are descendants of the original English, Germans, Scotch-Irish, and Africans who arrived in the 1700s. Today almost 5 percent of North Carolinians are of Hispanic origin, while slightly more than 1 percent are of Asian descent. North Carolinians born outside the United States come from countries such as the United Kingdom, Canada, Germany, Mexico, Korea, and Japan.

For every one hundred North Carolinians, about twenty-two are African American. This number has decreased from about thirty before World War II. At that time the "Jim

▲ The Qualla-Cherokee Indian Reservation, near Asheville, is the only site in North Carolina where the Cherokee were allowed to remain. Today the 56,000-acre (22,663-hectare) reservation attracts thousands of tourists each year.

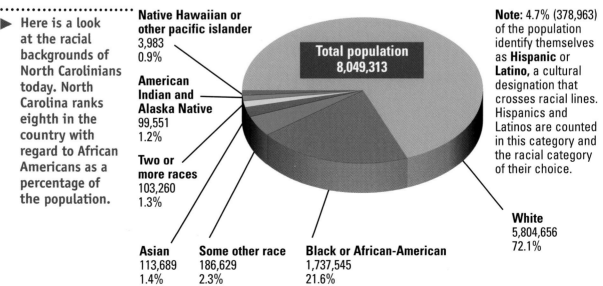

Heritage and Background, North Carolina — Year 2000

▶ Here is a look at the racial backgrounds of North Carolinians today. North Carolina ranks eighth in the country with regard to African Americans as a percentage of the population.

Native Hawaiian or other pacific islander
3,983
0.9%

American Indian and Alaska Native
99,551
1.2%

Two or more races
103,260
1.3%

Asian
113,689
1.4%

Some other race
186,629
2.3%

Black or African-American
1,737,545
21.6%

White
5,804,656
72.1%

Total population 8,049,313

Note: 4.7% (378,963) of the population identify themselves as **Hispanic** or **Latino,** a cultural designation that crosses racial lines. Hispanics and Latinos are counted in this category and the racial category of their choice.

Crow" laws formalizing segregation were still in effect. Large numbers of blacks left North Carolina during and after World War II to escape discrimination and unemployment.

The people of North Carolina historically have been as varied as the state's topography. Through the late 1800s farmers in the western mountains were isolated from the coastal planters and merchants because of the lack of transportation systems. Each region developed its own accents, dialects, and speech patterns, as well as preferences for different foods and ideas, giving North Carolina a rich culture and character. Today these regional distinctions are fading as roads and trains bring people from different parts of the state in contact with each other.

Educational Levels of North Carolina Workers

Less than 9th grade	539,974
9th to 12th grade, no diploma	737,773
High school graduate, including equivalency	1,232,868
Some college, no degree or associate degree	1,003,830
Bachelor's degree	510,003
Graduate or professional degree	229,046

▼ The modern skyline of Charlotte — North Carolina's most populous city.

Education

Education has been valued in North Carolina since its early days as a state. The state's first school opened in 1705. By 1846 there was at least one school in each county. More than half of state residents over the age of eighteen are high school graduates. Public school funding is the largest item in the state budget.

North Carolina's first school is believed to have been founded in 1705 in Symons Creek by Charles Griffin. At that time many people believed the church should control public education.

The establishment of a public school system was made possible by the state's Constitution of 1776. The Constitution also provided for the chartering of the University of North Carolina. When it opened its doors in 1795, it became the first state university in the country to hold classes. The University of North Carolina system now has sixteen campuses.

Private institutions of higher education include Duke University, Davidson College, Meredith College, and Wake Forest University.

Religion

Religion is an important part of life for many North Carolinians. Baptists form the largest religious group in North Carolina. Many North Carolinians are evangelicals who work to spread the word of the Bible. Billy Graham is a famous evangelist who was born in Charlotte and still lives in North Carolina. More than three-quarters of the people who live in North Carolina belong to Christian churches. Within this group the majority are Protestants, and nearly 50 percent of those Protestants are Baptists. Other Protestant groups in the state are members of Methodist, Presbyterian, Pentecostal, Lutheran, or African Methodist Episcopal Zion churches. Catholics make up about 3.2 percent of the population. Among those who do not belong to Christian churches, 0.3 percent are Jewish and 0.2 percent Muslim. North Carolina also has a small but growing Buddhist population.

Nature's Sample Case

> . . . an abundance of Deer and Turkies every where; we never going on shoar, but saw of each, also Partridges great store, Cranes abundance, Conies [rabbits], which we saw in several places; we heard several Wolfes howling in the woods, and saw where they had torn a Deer in pieces.
>
> — *William Hilton, 1664*

North Carolina is divided into three distinct geographic regions: the Atlantic Coastal Plain (or Tidewater) in the east; the Piedmont (from the Italian, meaning lying at the base of mountains), an area of gentle, rolling hills in the center; and the Mountain Region in the west. In addition, numerous sandbars and islands off the seacoast make up the Outer Banks.

The state's first town, Bath, was incorporated in the Coastal Plain region in 1705. This early settlement gave the region the description "The Cradle of North Carolina." The Coastal Plain covers the eastern two-fifths of the state. It is bordered by beaches and characterized by low marshland, swamps, vast wilderness areas, and grassy prairies. The Dismal Swamp, one of the country's largest swamps, and far from dismal, is located in the northeast coastal plain. Rich soil in the western coastal plain makes this area ideal for farming, as evidenced by the location of North Carolina's plantations in this region. Many of the

High Points

Mt. Mitchell
6,684 feet
(2,032 meters)

▼ *From left to right:* the old well at the University of North Carolina; a bridge across the Eno River; Cape Lookout; Wildflowers of North Carolina; Canoeing through Merchant's Mill Pond State Park; Grandfather Mountain.

state's main crops and forest-related products are produced here. The Coastal Plain meets the Piedmont at the Fall Line, where rivers rushing from the hilly Piedmont fall onto the grassy prairies below.

The hilly Piedmont rises from about 300 feet (91 m) at the Coastal Plain to an elevation of about 1,500 feet (457 m) where it meets the Blue Ridge Mountains in the west. This region is primarily a manufacturing area, in which the principal industries are tobacco, textiles, and furniture. Gold was discovered in the Piedmont region in 1799. It is home to the state's five largest cities — Charlotte, Raleigh, Greensboro, Winston-Salem, and Durham. More people live in the Piedmont than in the Coastal Plain and Mountain Regions combined.

The mountain ranges that make up North Carolina's Mountain Region are all part of the Appalachian Mountains, which stretch from Maine to Georgia. The Blue Ridge Mountains are the most prominent, but this region also includes the Great Smoky, Black, Bald, and Unaka Mountains. Forests cover most of the mountains and valleys; low hillsides provide more good farmland. In 2000 more tourists visited the Blue Ridge Parkway than any other site administered by the National Park Service.

The Outer Banks are a narrow chain of sandbars and small islands that form a nearly continuous barrier along the North Carolina coast. Where the Outer Banks jut into the Atlantic Ocean, they form the long, slender peninsulas of Cape Fear, Cape Lookout, and Cape Hatteras. As these names suggest, the shifting sands combined with swift currents made navigation difficult and dangerous for early explorers. So infamous were these waters that Cape Hatteras became known as "the Graveyard of the Atlantic."

Longest Rivers
Cape Fear River
103 miles (165 km)
Tar River
93 miles (149 km)
Yadkin River
89 miles (143 km)

Average January temperature range
Asheville: 27°–48°F (2.8°–8.9°C)
Wilmington: 36°–57°F (2.2°–13.9°C)

Average July temperature range
Asheville: 63°–84°F (17.2°–28.9°C)
Wilmington: 72°–89°F (22.2°–31.7°C)

Average yearly rainfall
Asheville: 45 inches (114 cm)
Wilmington: 54 inches (137 cm)

Average yearly snowfall
Asheville: 18 inches (46 cm)
Wilmington: 2 inches (5 cm)

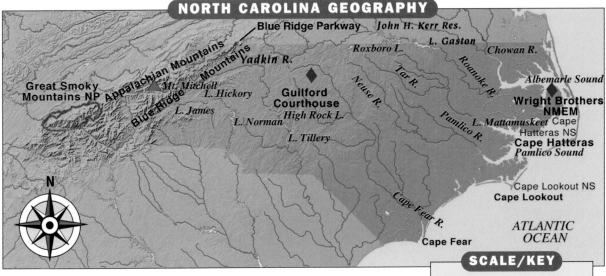

Blue Ridge Parkway — John H. Kerr Res.
L. Gaston
Roxboro L.
Chowan R.
Appalachian Mountains
Blue Ridge Mountains
Yadkin R.
Roanoke R.
Great Smoky
Mountains NP
Mt. Mitchell
L. Hickory
Guilford
Courthouse
High Rock L.
Albemarle Sound
Wright Brothers
NMEM
L. James
Neuse R.
Tar R.
Pamlico R.
L. Mattamuskeet Cape
Hatteras NS
Cape Hatteras
Pamlico Sound
L. Norman
L. Tillery
N
Cape Fear R.
Cape Lookout NS
Cape Lookout
ATLANTIC
OCEAN
Cape Fear

Rivers and Lakes

Most of North Carolina's rivers originate in the Mountain Region or the Piedmont. They flow southeastward and eventually empty into the Atlantic Ocean. Among the largest rivers are the Roanoke, Cape Fear, Chowan, Neuse, Tar, Yadkin, and Pamlico Rivers. The rivers change speed as they pass through the state's three major land regions. In the mountains the rivers are swift and create beautiful waterfalls. Across the rocky Piedmont the rivers have fast currents and narrow channels, again creating waterfalls and rapids at the Fall Line. Once in the Coastal Plain, they widen and flow more gracefully. One of the highest waterfalls in the eastern United States is Whitewater Falls, in southwestern North Carolina.

Plants

Despite the importance of the lumber industry, approximately two-thirds of North Carolina remains forest-covered. Because of North Carolina's varied geography, both subarctic (spruces and balsams) and subtropical (palmettos) species exist. Wildflowers color the North Carolina landscape in the spring. The southern coastal plain is host to such exotic plants as wild orchids and Venus's-flytraps (carnivorous plants that grow wild in only North and South Carolina).

SCALE/KEY

0	100 Miles
0	100 Km

◆ Landmark

▲ Highest Point

▨ Mountains

NMEM National Memorial

NP National Park

NS National Seashore

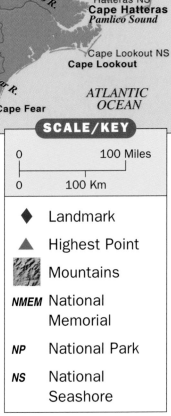

Great Smoky Mountains National Park

Within this park sixteen peaks rise to more than 6,000 feet (1,829 m). Mount Mitchell, at 6,684 feet (2,037 m), is the highest point in North Carolina and also the highest point east of the Mississippi River.

Animals

Deer roam throughout the state. Black bears live mainly in the Mountain Region and coastal lowlands. Smaller animals such as beavers, foxes, otters, rabbits, raccoons, skunks, and gray squirrels flourish in North Carolina's fields, forests, and streams. Birds common to the state include cardinals (the state bird), Carolina wrens, mockingbirds, mourning doves, partridges, and woodcocks. Winter brings huge flocks of ducks, geese, and swans to the coast. A small number of wild ponies still run free along the Outer Banks.

Climate

As North Carolina's geography varies, so does the state's climate. The Coastal Plain has the warmest winters and the hottest summers. Cooler weather reigns year-round in the Mountain Region, although the winters are still short and mild. The Piedmont climate, as might be expected, lies somewhere in between.

Despite these generally pleasant weather conditions, North Carolina gets its share of violent weather. In the past one hundred years, North Carolina has averaged nearly one hurricane a year. Residents still remember the hurricane of 1954, which killed nineteen people and caused more than $100 million worth of damages. In 1989 Hurricane Hugo killed two people and caused $1 billion in damage in North Carolina.

Lakes

North Carolina's natural lakes are small. Most, including the largest, Mattamuskeet, are in the Atlantic Coastal Plain. Several large artificial lakes have been formed by dams. These include John H. Kerr Reservoir and Lake Gaston, on the Roanoke River; High Rock Lake and Lake Tillery, on the Yadkin River; Lake Norman, on the Catawba River; and Fontana Lake, on the Little Tennessee River. A number of picturesque waterfalls are located in the Blue Ridge region.

Largest Lakes

John H. Kerr Reservoir
48,900 acres
(19,790 ha)

Lake Mattamuskeet
40,000 acres
(16,000 ha)

Lake Norman
32,510 acres
(13,157 ha)

High Rock Lake
15,250 acres
(6,172 ha)

◀ A house in Wilmington burns in the aftermath of Hurricane Hazel, in 1954. North Carolina averages about one hurricane each year.

From Tar to the Triangle

> That with prudent Management, I can affirm, by Experience, not by Hear-say, That any Person, with a small Beginning, may live very comfortably, and not only provide for the Necessaries of Life, but likewise for those that are to succeed him.
>
> — *John Lawson, British Surveyor-General of North Carolina, 1700*

Through the colonial period North Carolina's major industry was the production of naval supplies, namely tar, pitch, and turpentine. This is the most commonly accepted explanation for the state's nickname — "Tar Heel State." This lumber-based industry was concentrated in the coastal region. In the Piedmont and western mountains, largely self-sufficient farmers were growing the crops, weaving the cloth, and building the furniture that later would make the state a leader in agriculture and manufacturing. A poor transportation system kept North Carolina's commerce behind other states until after the Civil War. Once roads and railroad tracks were laid, North Carolina went full-steam ahead. Factories, textile mills, and tobacco-processing plants sprang up all over the state and revolutionized the once mainly rural state.

Agriculture

About one-third of the Tar Heel State is farmland. Livestock products and crops each account for about half of the state's agricultural income.

Tobacco is North Carolina's most valuable agricultural product. About 40 percent of U.S. tobacco is grown in North Carolina. Tobacco is grown throughout the state, but most is grown in the Coastal Plain and Mountain Region. More fire-cured tobacco is sold in Wilson, North Carolina, than in any other city in the country.

North Carolina cultivates more sweet potatoes than any

Top Employers
(of workers age sixteen and over; totals add up to more than 100% as some residents may hold two or more jobs)

Services	33.0%
Manufacturing	26.0%
Wholesale and retail trade	20.0%
Government	14.0%
Construction	7.0%
Transportation, communications and other public utilities	6.2%
Finance, insurance, and real estate	5.0%
Agriculture, forestry, and fisheries	2.7%
Mining	0.2%

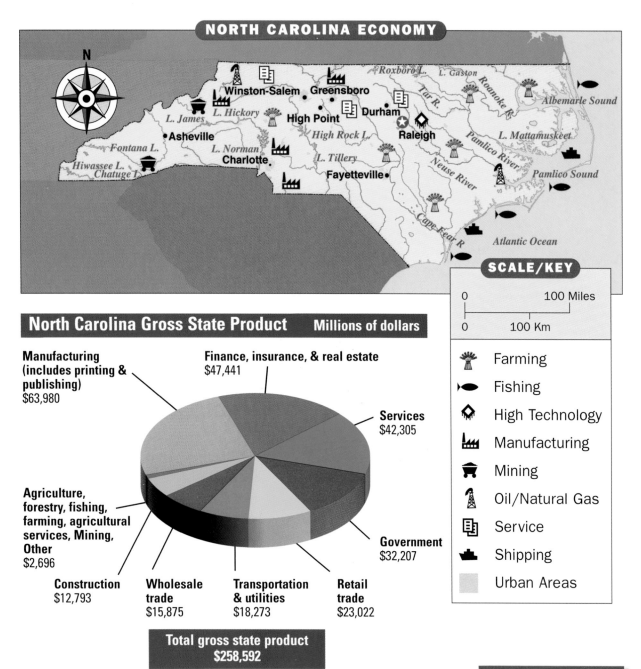

NORTH CAROLINA ECONOMY

North Carolina Gross State Product — Millions of dollars

Manufacturing (includes printing & publishing) $63,980

Finance, insurance, & real estate $47,441

Services $42,305

Government $32,207

Retail trade $23,022

Transportation & utilities $18,273

Wholesale trade $15,875

Construction $12,793

Agriculture, forestry, fishing, farming, agricultural services, Mining, Other $2,696

Total gross state product $258,592

SCALE/KEY

0 — 100 Miles
0 — 100 Km

- Farming
- Fishing
- High Technology
- Manufacturing
- Mining
- Oil/Natural Gas
- Service
- Shipping
- Urban Areas

other state; it should come as no surprise that the sweet potato is North Carolina's state vegetable. Also, more turkeys are raised in North Carolina than anywhere else in the United States. Hogs, however, provide the most income of all the state's livestock products.

Natural Resources

North Carolina relies on and makes excellent use of its thick forests, rich soils, and mineral deposits to support its

industries. Forests cover two-thirds of the state and are the state's greatest natural resource. A greater variety of trees grow in North Carolina than in any other state except Florida and Texas. Oaks and pines are the most common species. North Carolina leads the states in the production of hardwood veneer and hardwood plywood, as well as being a national leader in commercial forests reserves. The forestry industry in North Carolina is replenishing the supply of trees cut down for business, rather than simply clear-cutting.

North Carolina's soil contains more than three hundred different minerals and rocks, giving the state the name "Nature's Sample Case." The Piedmont and Mountain Regions contain rubies, sapphires, emeralds, and even diamonds, in addition to less glamorous minerals such as feldspar, kaolin, and gneiss. Limestone is the state's leading mineral product. North Carolina is the country's major source of mica.

▲ North Carolina has a diverse economy. It leads the nation in the production of textiles, while its fishermen bring in an annual catch worth about $100 million.

Manufacturing

Manufacturing is the single most important economic activity in North Carolina. It accounts for a larger portion of gross state product than in most other states. Approximately one-fourth of the state's employees work in the manufacturing sector.

In terms of value added by manufacturing, chemicals rank number one among North Carolina's manufactured products. The main chemical products are pharmaceuticals (medicines) and synthetic fibers. Raleigh, Kingston, and Shelby are home to major chemical plants.

The state is most famous for its second most important manufactured product — tobacco. North Carolina is the top producer of tobacco in the United States. About half of the country's cigarettes are produced in factories in Greensboro, Reidsville, and Winston-Salem. The success of North Carolina's tobacco industry may be attributed to Buck Duke, who founded the American Tobacco Company in 1890. Duke later donated $40 million to Trinity College, which was renamed Duke University.

Textiles are the third most important manufactured product, and include sheets, towels, and carpeting. North Carolina leads not only the United States but most other nations in the production of textiles.

Furniture is also one of North Carolina's most important manufactured products. Drawing on the state's vast hardwood and softwood forests, North Carolina factories lead the nation's production of household furniture. North Carolina's furniture industry began in the late 1800s in High Point, which is often referred to as the "Furniture Capital of the World."

Located in the triangle between Raleigh, Durham, and Chapel Hill, Research Triangle Park is a large research complex that houses many medical and research laboratories. It was founded in 1959 by Duke University, the University of North Carolina at Chapel Hill, and North Carolina State University to support industry. Companies such as IBM and GlaxoSmithKline have a presence in this complex.

▲ North Carolina's state vegetable — the sweet potato — was grown in the area long before European settlement. The sweet potato is not actually a potato. It is the root of a plant in the morning glory family.

Made in North Carolina

Leading farm products and crops
Tobacco
Corn
Soybeans
Chickens
Hogs
Turkeys

Other products
Clothes and textiles
Industrial machinery
Electronic equipment
Furniture and fixtures

A State of Resolve

> It is slavery which, more than any other cause,
> keeps us back in the career of improvement
>
> — *Judge Gaston*

N orth Carolina has had three state Constitutions over the course of its history. Important revisions were made to the state's original 1776 Constitution in 1835. The revisions gave greater political representation to people in North Carolina's western regions and stimulated the development of business and cultural activities there. A new state Constitution, put forth in 1868, abolished slavery and gave African Americans the vote. The present Constitution went into effect in 1971.

The state government of North Carolina is comprised of three branches: the executive, which carries out laws; the legislative, which writes new laws and repeals old laws; and the judicial, which interprets laws and presides over cases.

The Executive Branch

The executive branch is headed by the governor. The governor and lieutenant governor are elected to four-year

Independence Resolution

Resolved that the delegates for this Colony in the Continental Congress be empowered to concur with the other delegates of the other Colonies in declaring Independency . . .

From the Halifax Resolves, April 12, 1776. North Carolina thereby became the first colony to authorize a declaration of independence from Great Britain.

Elected Posts in the Executive Branch

Office	Length of Term	Term Limits
Governor	4 years	2 consecutive terms in 12 years
Lieutenant Governor	4 years	2 consecutive terms in 12 years
Secretary of State	4 years	None
Attorney General	4 years	None
Auditor	4 years	None
Superintendent of Public Instruction	4 years	None
Treasurer	4 years	None
Commissioners of Agriculture, Labor, and Insurance	4 years	None

terms. The governor has the power to appoint a number of important state officials, head the budget bureau, and call out the state armed forces in times of emergency. In 1996 the state's Constitution was amended to give the governor the power to veto laws written by the state legislature. The council of state, an advisory council to the governor, consists of the executive branch's elected officials.

The General Assembly

The legislative branch is called the General Assembly. It is made up of a 50-member Senate and a 120-member House of Representatives. Members of both houses are elected by the voters to serve two-year terms. The lieutenant governor presides over the Senate. The House of Representatives elects its own president. The General Assembly meets every year. The main responsibility of the General Assembly is to debate proposed laws (or bills). A bill becomes law when a majority of the members vote for it.

The Judicial Branch

The Supreme Court is the highest court in North Carolina's judicial system. It consists of a chief justice and six associate justices. All of these judges are elected to eight-year terms. The second-most powerful court is the court of appeals, which has a chief judge and eleven associate judges. Judges in the court of appeals also serve eight-year terms. The superior and district courts hear a wide range of cases.

Local Government

North Carolina's one hundred counties each are governed by a board of county commissioners. The state grants cities

◄ The North Carolina State Capitol was completed in 1840.

and towns home rule or self-government, enabling them to make certain amendments to their charters. They remain under the control of the General Assembly, however.

Running the state government is a very expensive business. For example, funding the public school system costs the government more than $2 billion a year. The government raises about 60 percent of its revenue through taxation. The government also receives grants from the federal government to fund important activities.

▲ The Executive Mansion for North Carolina's governor was completed in 1891. It is a fine example of the "Queen Anne" style of architecture.

A Struggle

In the late 1800s there was great struggle between Republicans and Democrats. The Ku Klux Klan, which supported white supremacy, backed the Democratic Party. In 1870 the Democrats gained control of the state legislature. They impeached Republican Governor William Holden in 1871, removing him from office. He was the first governor ever to be impeached in North Carolina. In 1875 the Democratic legislature added thirty amendments to the Constitution that ensured white, Democratic control of county government. In 1898 the Democrats amended the state Constitution again to deprive blacks of voting rights, and to enact new laws requiring racial segregation of schools, trains, and other public facilities.

The Democratic Party dominated the political scene in North Carolina through the mid-1900s. In modern times, however, the tables have turned. The Republican presidential candidate won North Carolina's electoral votes only once (in 1928) between 1865 and 1964. Since 1968, however, the Republican has been victorious in all but one presidential election (1976). In 1972 James Holshouser, Jr., was the first Republican to be elected governor since 1896. That same year Jesse Helms became the first Republican elected to the U.S. Senate from North Carolina since 1895.

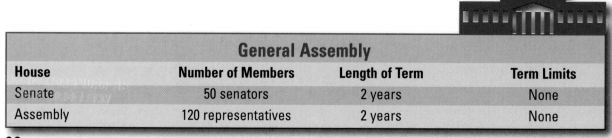

General Assembly			
House	Number of Members	Length of Term	Term Limits
Senate	50 senators	2 years	None
Assembly	120 representatives	2 years	None

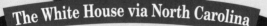

Three men from North Carolina have served as president of the United States — though all three were elected while residents of Tennessee.

ANDREW JACKSON (1829–1837)

Jackson was born in the Waxhaws area near the border between North and South Carolina on March 15, 1767. Jackson's parents lived in North Carolina, but historians are not really sure on which side of the state line he was born. Union County in North Carolina and Lancaster County in South Carolina have come up with their own solution. Their high school football teams play each other annually in the "Old Hickory Classic." The winning county adopts Jackson as a native son for the following year. Jackson was the first man elected from Tennessee to the House of Representatives, and he served briefly in the Senate. A general in the War of 1812, Jackson became a national hero when he defeated the British at New Orleans. National politics eventually polarized around Jackson — for and against. Two parties grew out of the old Jeffersonian Republican Party — the Democrats, adhering to Jackson; and the National Republicans, or Whigs, opposing him. Both Jackson and Whig leaders proclaimed themselves defenders of popular liberties. Hostile cartoonists portrayed Jackson as King Andrew I.

JAMES KNOX POLK (1845–1849)

Born in Mecklenburg County, North Carolina, in 1795, Polk was educated in North Carolina, but began his career in Tennessee. He served as Speaker of the House of Representatives between 1835 and 1839, leaving to become Governor of Tennessee. At the 1844 Democratic Convention Polk was nominated on the ninth ballot as the "Dark Horse" candidate for president. Whigs jeered: "Who is James K. Polk?" Democrats replied that Polk was the candidate who stood for expansion. Committed to the nation's "Manifest Destiny," Polk added a vast area to the United States during his presidency. He was the last of the Jacksonians to sit in the White House before the Civil War.

ANDREW JOHNSON (1865–1869)

Born in Raleigh, North Carolina, in 1808, Johnson grew up in poverty. He moved to Tennessee and became a tailor before entering politics. A U.S. senator from Tennessee, he remained in the Senate even when his state seceded from the Union. That made him a hero in the North and a traitor in the eyes of most southerners. In 1862 President Abraham Lincoln appointed him Military Governor of Tennessee, and Johnson used the state as a laboratory for reconstruction. In 1864 the Republicans, contending that their National Union Party was for all loyal men, nominated Johnson, a southerner and a Democrat, for vice president. He became president after the assassination of Abraham Lincoln. Johnson was the first president to be impeached, though it is now widely acknowledged that the impeachment was for political rather than ethical reasons. The House voted eleven articles of impeachment against him. He was tried by the Senate in the spring of 1868 and acquitted by one vote.

Mountains to Museums

> Then let all those who love us, love the land that we live in, As happy a region as on this side of heaven, Where plenty and peace, love and joy smile before us
>
> — *William Gaston, "The Old North State," North Carolina's state song*

N orth Carolina's mountains, beaches, and historic sites offer a tremendous variety of recreational opportunities. With two national seashores, the beautiful Great Smoky Mountains National Park, sixty-six Revolutionary War sites, one of the largest zoos in the world, and some of the country's most beautiful estates, there is something for everyone in the Tar Heel State.

Leisure in Art

Art has been a part of everyday life in North Carolina for more than three centuries. During the Colonial period, women wove beautiful cloth on homemade looms, while men carved furniture and other household items. Even though these items were functional, they were also works of art. Variety is particularly evident in the state's musical offerings. Every year thousands of classical music lovers attend concerts performed by the North Carolina Symphony Orchestra. Gospel and country music are very popular in North Carolina, as are folk and bluegrass. North Carolina has produced a number of famous musicians, including bluegrass musician Earl Scruggs, saxophonist John Coltrane, and Roberta Flack, a popular singer in the 1970s.

One of the South's most prestigious art museums is the North Carolina Museum of Art, which opened in Raleigh in 1956. The University of North Carolina also maintains two excellent art museums.

The most distinctive feature of North Carolina's theater scene is the presentation of historical dramas. These plays, which often are accompanied by music and dancing, focus on key events in the state's history and usually are performed outdoors. The most famous and longest-running of these performances is *The Lost Colony*, which portrays some of the hardships faced by the early English colonists who disappeared from Roanoke Island in the late 1500s.

Libraries and Museums

The first public library in North Carolina was founded in about 1700 by an English missionary named Thomas Bray. Today North Carolina has an extensive public library system as well as several cooperative library organizations that allow for the sharing of books. The largest collections of books in the state are housed in the libraries at Duke University and the University of North Carolina at Chapel Hill. These libraries include extensive collections of documents on southern history and culture.

The history of North Carolina is the focus of the Greensboro Historical Museum (which houses an exhibit on the famous civil rights "sit-in" of 1960) and the North Carolina Museum of History in Raleigh.

The Mint Museum of Art in Charlotte is located in a building that was the United States government mint in the mid-1800s. The museum displays gold coins from the days when the government turned North Carolina's gold into currency.

▲ Franklin Street, near the University of North Carolina at Chapel Hill.

Outdoor Theater

North Carolina has a tradition of outdoor theater. The most famous is the Waterside Theater in Manteo, which since 1937 has been the home of *The Lost Colony*. One of the oldest outdoor plays in the country, *The Lost Colony* is an interpretation of one of American history's great mysteries: the disappearance of settlers on Roanoke Island.

The Morehead Planetarium, with a dome spanning 68 feet (20.7 meters), is located at the University of North Carolina at Chapel Hill. The North Carolina Museum of Natural Sciences in Raleigh has an impressive collection of dinosaurs and other animals on display.

Visitors to the North Carolina Zoological Park, near Asheboro, can see over seven hundred animals and more than thirty thousand species of plants. It is one of the nation's largest walk-through natural-habitat zoos.

The Biltmore Estate was built near Asheville in the 1890s for millionaire George Vanderbilt, one of the country's wealthiest men. With 250 rooms, it is the largest private home in America.

Tryon Palace is considered to be one of colonial America's prettiest buildings. Built by William Tryon, a royal governor, Tryon Palace originally was the governor's mansion. American patriots met in the palace in 1774 in defiance of

▼ **The North Carolina Zoological Park, the nation's first state-supported zoo, is home to these two Southern White Rhinos.**

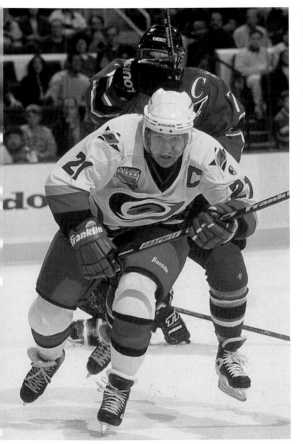

British authority and went so far as to make it the seat of the capitol of North Carolina during the Revolutionary War.

Lexington, North Carolina, is Barbecue Capital of the World. There are twenty barbecue restaurants in this Piedmont town of twenty thousand. Each year since 1984 the town hosts a two day barbecue festival on one of the last weekends in October, Barbecue Month. Hickory smoked pork barbecue basted with "dip" — a mixture of vinegar, water, salt, and pepper — is sold in three tents during the festival. This is typical southern barbecue, while Texas style barbecue is famous for ribs and a thick, tangy sauce. The festival also features a bicycle race known as the Tour de Pig, and events in golfing, tennis, and gymnastics.

Sports

In terms of sports, North Carolina may be best known for its successes in college basketball. The Duke University Blue Devils have won three NCAA championships and have made that competition's Final Four nine times. Coach Mike Krzyzewski was inducted into the Basketball Hall of Fame

Sport	Team	Home
Basketball	Charlotte Hornets	Charlotte Coliseum, Charlotte
Football	Carolina Panthers	Ericsson Stadium, Charlotte
Hockey	Carolina Hurricanes	Entertainment and Sports Arena, Raleigh

for his excellent coaching of the Duke team. The University of North Carolina at Chapel Hill (the North Carolina Tar Heels) and North Carolina State University also field top teams almost every year. Michael Jordan attended the University of North Carolina at Chapel Hill.

Professional sports teams from North Carolina include the Charlotte Hornets basketball team and the Carolina Hurricanes hockey team. The movie *Bull Durham* made the minor league Durham Bulls baseball team famous.

Golfers flock to North Carolina for its beautiful golf courses and the World Golf Hall of Fame in Pinehurst.

Auto racing is popular in North Carolina. Some of the sport's big events, including the National 500, are held every year at the state's two major racetracks.

The National Association for Stock Car Auto Racing held its first official race in Daytona, Florida, in 1948, but the sport really began on the dirt roads of North Carolina. Junior Johnson, one of the sport's earliest heroes, developed his knack for speed while transporting moonshine

▼ On February 25, 2001, NASCAR driver Jeff Gordon (car 24), leaves the pole position open during a pace lap of the Dura-Lube 400 at the North Carolina Raceway in Rockingham. He did so in honor of Dale Earnhardt, Sr., who had died the previous week.

(homemade liquor made from corn) on the back roads of North Carolina. Many NASCAR records have been established at the North Carolina Speedway in Rockingham, where driving speeds can exceed 150 miles (241 kilometers) per hour. Richard Petty, who has won more races than any other driver in NASCAR history (200) and who is known as "the King," is from Level Cross.

Historic Sites

One of North Carolina's most famous attractions is the battleship U.S.S. *North Carolina,* which participated in every major battle in the Pacific Ocean during World War II. Visitors may tour the battleship, located on the Cape Fear River at Wilmington.

The first powered airplane flight is honored at the Wright Brothers National Memorial at Kill Devil Hills, near Kitty Hawk. Today hang gliders and kite fliers come to the area to take advantage of the same strong winds that in 1903 helped Orville and Wilbur Wright launch their famous flight.

Visitors to the Reed Gold Mine near Charlotte can pan for gold much like people did in the 1800s. The mine, now a museum and tourist attraction, was started by the family of Conrad Reed, who found a huge gold nugget on his farm in 1799 and started the country's first gold rush.

A replica of a Native American village in the state's mountain region provides a glimpse of early Cherokee life. At the Oconaluftee Indian Village (or Cherokee Indian Reservation) in Cherokee, visitors can see demonstrations of Cherokee arts and crafts.

History enthusiasts may visit the site of the Regulators' rebellion at Alamance Battlefield, near Burlington, and the Bentonville Battlefield, the site of one of the last important battles of the Civil War.

▼ Wright Brothers National Memorial at Kill Devil Hills, near Kitty Hawk.

High Fliers

The fact is that the character of her people, most admirable climate
and the opportunities afforded by her extraordinarily varied resources,
are at the bottom of it all.

— *Alex Graham, Scenes of North Carolina, 1895*

Following are only a few of the thousands who lived, died, or spent most of their lives in
North Carolina while making extraordinary contributions to the state and the nation.

VIRGINIA DARE

PIONEER

BORN: *August 18, 1587, Roanoke Island
(then Virginia, now North Carolina)*
DIED: *unknown*

Dare was the first child born to English parents in the Americas. Her fate is unknown as she was born into the ill-fated "Lost Colony" of Roanoke Island. Her mother, Ellinor White Dare, was the daughter of the Roanoke Colony governor, John White.

BLACKBEARD

PIRATE

BORN: *circa 1680, Bristol, England*
DIED: *November 22, 1718, Ocracoke Island*

Edward Teach, known as Blackbeard, was the most infamous pirate to frequent the islands along North Carolina's Outer Banks. He is believed to have lived on Ocracoke island at one time, and to have married a young woman there. He was killed off the coast of Ocracoke on November 22, 1718, by British Lieutenant Robert Maynard, and his severed head hung from the bowsprit of Maynard's ship as a warning to other pirates.

DOLLEY MADISON
FIRST LADY

BORN: *May 20, 1768, Guilford County*
DIED: *July 12, 1849, Washington, D.C.*

Dolley Payne was the wife of James Madison, who became president of the United States in 1809. One of America's most famous first ladies, she held the title for sixteen years. When her husband was Thomas Jefferson's vice president, she served as the White House hostess because Jefferson's wife had died. She served another eight years during her husband's two terms as president. She is remembered for originating the annual Easter Egg Roll on the White House lawn and for saving George Washington's portrait and important state documents when the British set the White House on fire during the War of 1812.

HIRAM RHOADES REVELS
POLITICIAN AND STATESMAN

BORN: *September 1, 1822, Fayetteville*
DIED: *January 16, 1901, Aberdeen, MS*

Revels was born a free black person. He became a minister and helped to establish black churches and schools. During the Civil War, Revels helped form black units for the Union army. In 1870 Revels became the first black U.S. senator when he was elected to represent the state of Mississippi.

O. HENRY
WRITER

BORN: *September 11, 1862, Greensboro*
DIED: *June 5, 1910, New York, NY*

William Sydney Porter grew up in North Carolina during the Reconstruction era. He dropped out of school when he was about fifteen and was later jailed for stealing money from a bank where he had worked. From his prison cell, he wrote a number of short stories under the pen name O. Henry. In total, O. Henry wrote about 250 pieces of short fiction, including "The Gift of the Magi."

THOMAS WOLFE
WRITER

BORN: *October 3, 1900, Asheville*
DIED: *September 15, 1938, Baltimore, MD*

Wolfe was a world-famous novelist. His *Look Homeward, Angel* is an autobiographical novel about life in a small town. Wolfe's other novels include *You Can't Go Home Again* and *Of Time and the River.*

BILLY GRAHAM
EVANGELIST

BORN: *November 7, 1918, Charlotte*

Born on a farm near Charlotte, Graham is probably the most famous evangelical preacher in the world. Reverend Graham has preached to millions of people worldwide, advised several presidents, and written many books.

WILBUR WRIGHT

INVENTOR AND AVIATOR

BORN: *April 16, 1867, near Millville, IN*
DIED: *May 30, 1912, Dayton, OH*

ORVILLE WRIGHT

INVENTOR AND AVIATOR

BORN: *August 19, 1871, Dayton, OH*
DIED: *January 30, 1948, Dayton, OH*

On December 17, 1903, the Wright brothers put North Carolina's Outer Banks on the international map. They made the first successful manned and powered airplane flight, lasting only twelve seconds and covering just 120 feet (37 m). The first flight was made near Kitty Hawk, at Kill Devil Hills, where a national monument was erected in honor of the Wright brothers.

ELIZABETH DOLE

STATESWOMAN

BORN: *July 29, 1936, Salisbury*

Dole, known as Liddy, is a graduate of Duke University. In 1983 she became the first woman U.S. Secretary of Transportation, and in 1989 she became Secretary of Labor under President George Bush. As secretary of labor, she started the "Glass Ceiling Study" to find out why women were prevented from getting senior management jobs. In 1999 Dole ran an unsuccessful campaign for the Republican presidential nomination. She was also the first woman to serve as president of the American Red Cross (1991–1999) since the organization's founder, Clara Barton, held the position in 1881.

▼ The historic flight at Kill Devil Hills.

DALE EARNHARDT
PROFESSIONAL NASCAR DRIVER

BORN: *April 29, 1951, Kannapolis*
DIED: *February 19, 2001, Daytona, FL*

Ralph Dale Earnhardt's father raced in stock-car races, and young Dale became a racing enthusiast early on. By his late teens Dale was working full-time as a mechanic and using his pay to get his racing career started. His first National Association for Stock Car Auto Racing (NASCAR) win came in 1980, when Dale was twenty-nine years old. From that point on, no one could catch him. That same year he was named Rookie of the Year, and the following year he was the NASCAR series champion, the only person to win both titles back-to-back. He went on to win nearly every major event and title available to NASCAR drivers, including the Daytona 500. His career ended tragically with a fatal car accident at the Daytona 500 in 2001.

"SUGAR RAY" LEONARD
BOXER

BORN: *May 17, 1956, Rocky Mount*

Ray Charles Leonard won an Olympic gold medal and five world boxing titles. He was inducted into the International Boxing Hall of Fame in 1997.
After his retirement the popular Leonard worked as a sports commentator on television.

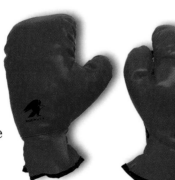

THELONIOUS MONK
COMPOSER AND MUSICIAN

BORN: *October 11, 1918, Rocky Mount*
DIED: *February 17, 1982, Weehawken, NJ*

One of the greatest and most innovative jazz musicians of all time, Thelonious Sphere Monk is credited as one of the creators of modern jazz. He started playing the piano at age five, when he was living in New York City, but did not begin formal lessons until he was eleven or twelve. After an early start touring as the musical accompanist to an evangelist, he briefly attended the Juilliard School of Music in New York City, but left to start a jazz career, playing with the jazz greats of the day. His shy manner kept his career from taking off, but he continued to write and play some of his most famous compositions. In 1955, however, he signed with Riverside Records. An album he made with John Coltrane in 1957 helped make him one of jazz's great celebrities. Unfortunately, Monk suffered from mental illness and retired from public life in 1973.

North Carolina

History At-A-Glance

1524
Giovanni da Verrazano, an Italian explorer sailing for France, visits the North Carolina coast.

1585
The English establish their first colony in what is now the United States at Roanoke Island.

ca. 1650
The first permanent settlers came to the Albemarle region from Virginia.

1677
Culpeper's Rebellion occurs, in which colonists rebel against the colonial governor.

1776
North Carolina delegates to the Continental Congress become the first to be instructed to vote for independence from England; the Whigs defeat the Tories at Moore's Creek Bridge; North Carolina adopts its first constitution.

1789
North Carolina ratifies the Constitution and joins the Union as the 12th state on November 21.

1540
Spanish explorer Hernando de Soto crosses the mountains of western North Carolina.

1587
A second group of settlers arrives at Roanoke; Virginia Dare is born.

1664
North Carolina's first permanent government is established in Albemarle County.

1729
North Carolina comes under direct royal rule after the lords' proprietors sell back their land.

1799
The first significant deposit of gold in the United States is discovered.

1600	1700	1800

1492
Christopher Columbus comes to New World.

1607
Capt. John Smith and three ships land on Virginia coast and start first English settlement in Americas — Jamestown.

1754–63
French and Indian Wars.

1773
Boston Tea Party.

1776
Declaration of Independence adopted July 4.

1777
Articles of Confederation adopted by Continental Congress.

1787
U.S. Constitution written.

1812–14
War of 1812.

United States

History At-A-Glance

1903
The Wright brothers make the first successful powered airplane flight near Kitty Hawk.

1984
Senator Jesse Helms defeats former governor Jim Hunt in the most expensive Senate election in the country's history.

1865
General Joseph E. Johnston surrenders to Union General William T. Sherman near Durham.

1960
A small group of black students launch the "sit-in" movement at a lunch counter in Greensboro to protest segregation.

1915
The State Highway Commission is formed and begins an extensive road-building program; as a result, North Carolina earns recognition as the "Good Roads State."

1989
North Carolina celebrates the bicentennial (200th anniversary) of its statehood; Hurricane Hugo causes $1 billion worth of damage in North Carolina and kills at least two people.

1840
The state's first railroad is completed, linking Wilmington to Weldon.

1917–18
Nearly 100,000 North Carolinians serve in World War I.

1868
North Carolina is readmitted to the Union and adopts a new state constitution.

1972
James E. Holshouser, Jr., becomes the first Republican to be elected governor of North Carolina since 1896.

1861
North Carolina secedes from the Union.

1941–45
About 400,000 Tar Heels serve in World War II.

1800 — **1900** — **2000**

1848
Gold discovered in California draws 80,000 prospectors in the 1849 Gold Rush.

1869
Transcontinental Railroad completed.

1929
Stock market crash ushers in Great Depression.

1950–53
U.S. fights in the Korean War.

2000
George W. Bush wins the closest presidential election in history.

1917–18
U.S. involvement in World War I.

1941–45
U.S. involvement in World War II.

1964–73
U.S. involvement in Vietnam War.

1861–65
Civil War.

2001
A terrorist attack in which four hijacked airliners crash into New York City's World Trade Center, the Pentagon, and farmland in western Pennsylvania leaves thousands dead or injured.

▼ A view of Raleigh, North Carolina's capital, circa 1909.

Festivals and Fun For All

Check web sites for exact dates and directions.

African-American Arts Festival, Greensboro

A celebration of the outstanding contributions that African-American artists have made to U.S. culture.

www.greensboro.com/arts/aaaf.html

Appalachian Summer Festival, Boone

Music, visual arts, theater, workshops, lectures, and more.

appsummer.highsouth.com

Azalea Festival, Wilmington

For fifty years, the folks of southeastern North Carolina have thrown "the best party you've ever seen." They invite the whole world to come "sit a spell."

www.azalea.wilmington.org/index.php

Barbecue Festival, Lexington

Lexington is home to legendary southern barbecue, but this festival also offers exhibits and entertainment.

www.barbecuefestival.com

Cape Fear Blues Festival, Wilmington

Blues enthusiasts join together to create a rockin' good time for all.

www.capefearblues.com

Dixie Classic Fair, Winston-Salem

The Dixie Classic Fair began as a grain exhibition in Salem in 1882. Now it features livestock entries, a carnival midway, and a collection of buildings from the 1800s.

www.dcfair.com

Folk Festival, Waynesville

Musicians from more than ten countries travel to North Carolina to create great music on unique instruments. Held in the cool, green mountains of the Great Smoky Mountains National Park.

www.folkmoot.com

Hillsborough Hog Day, Hillsborough

A barbecue contest, live music, children's rides, vintage and antique car show, arts and crafts, and more. (Don't miss the "best-dressed" pig contest.)

www.southfest.com/festivals/
hillsboroughhog.shtml

North Carolina Apple Festival, Hendersonville

More than 150 vendors line six blocks of historic Hendersonville while bands entertain the crowds with gospel, bluegrass, beach, and folk music.

www.ncapplefestival.org

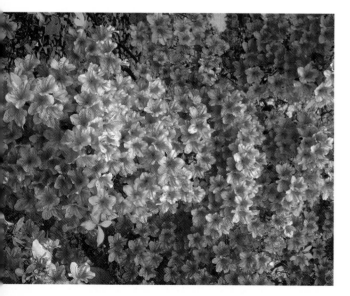

◀ Southerners love azaleas.

North Carolina Oyster Festival, Ocean Isle Beach

Enjoy live entertainment, arts, crafts, food, children's activities, and lots of fun.
www.oibgov.com/oysterfest.htm

North Carolina Pickle Festival, Mount Olive

Music, classic cars, games, food, and fun for all!
www.ncpicklefest.org

North Carolina Turkey Festival, Raeford

North Carolina is a national leader in turkey farming, and the Turkey Festival features everything festival-goers care to gobble up — free non-stop music and entertainment and an outstanding display of North Carolina arts and crafts.
www.hoke-raeford.com/nctf.htm

▲ For the love of turkey.

North Carolina Strawberry Festival, Chadbourn

Attractions, dinners, dances, bands, clowns, and strawberry shortcake galore!
www.ncstrawberryfestival.com

State Fair, Raleigh

Check out the monthly calendar of events for fun year-round.
www.ncstatefair.org/events/calendar.htm

Riverrun International Film Festival, Brevard

Not just a film festival — there's art, music, social events, poetry, film, and workshops.
www.riverrunfilm.com

Tweetsie Railroad Ghost Train Halloween Festival, Blowing Rock

Take a night ride on a Ghost Train at this spooky festival that promises fun for everyone.
www.tweetsie.com/ghosttrain.html

◄ Rides and more at the State Fair.

Books

Barnes, Jay. *North Carolina's Hurricane History.* Chapel Hill, NC: University of North Carolina Press, 2001. The East Coast of the United States is buffeted by hurricanes, and at times North Carolina has born the brunt. A fascinating history.

Dial, Adolph L. *The Lumbee.* New York: Chelsea House, 1993. Explore the rich history of the Native Americans who lived in North Carolina before European settlement.

Earley, Lawrence S. *North Carolina Wild Places: A Closer Look.* Raleigh, NC: North Carolina Wildlife Resources Commission, 1994. Get to know the plants, animals and terrain of North Carolina's wilderness areas.

Kelly, Fred C., et al. *Miracle at Kitty Hawk: The Letters of Wilbur and Orville Wright.* Scranton, PA: Da Capo Press, 1996. Letters the Wright Brothers wrote as they worked towards their famous achievement.

King, Casey. *Oh, Freedom!: Kids Talk About the Civil Rights Movement With the People Who Made It Happen.* New York: Knopf, 1997. Childrens' interviews with family and friends about their roles in the civil rights movement.

Milton, Douglas, editor, et al. The North Carolina Atlas: Portrait for a New Century. Chapel Hill, NC: University of North Carolina Press, 2000. A wealth of up-to-date information about the state.

Weatherford, Carol Boston. *Sink or Swim: African-American Lifesavers of the Outer Banks.* Wilmington, NC: Coastal Carolina Press, 1999. The history of the only all-black squad in the U.S. Lifesaving Service who operated off of Pea Island along the coast of North Carolina. The U.S. Lifesaving Service was a precursor to the Coast Guard.

Web Sites

▶ The official state site
www.ncgov.com

▶ The official site of Raleigh, North Carolina's capital
www.raleigh-nc.org

▶ The North Carolina Encyclopedia
statelibrary.dcr.state.nc.us/nc/cover.htm

▶ The American Memory Collection Finder: Search the Library of Congress for original material about North Carolina and the rest of the United States
memory.loc.gov/ammen/collections/finder.html

Note: Page numbers in *italics* refer to illustrations or photographs.